The Key Person Approach

Positive Relationships in the Early Years

by Jennie Lindon

Published by Practical P...
Tel: 020 7738 5454 ww...
© MA Education Ltd 20...   ...ation Ltd.

Referencing
- In text
  - Lindon (2012:pg)
- Bibliography
  - Lindon, J. (2012) The Key Person Approach, London: Practical Pre-School Books

A focus on positive relationships

The early years of a child's life are especially important: the quality of those experiences set the scene for the future. Young children build a set of expectations about their personal world and their place in it. Over early childhood they need to have developed strong, affectionate, sustained relationships with a small number of people. Children's first and most enduring bond is within their own family. However, a high proportion of young children in the UK spend time – sometimes a significant amount of time – as the responsibility of non-family adults, within the different types of early years group provision and the childminding service.

The development of attachment

Babies and very young children need to develop secure emotional attachment to familiar figures over their early childhood. Strong, sustained emotional bonds are the foundations for healthy development. This section offers a brief description of a complex area of practical research; you will find more detail in Lindon (2012 and 2012a) and Elfer et al. (2003).

There is very good reason to be concerned if circumstances mean that babies and very young children do not make a strong emotional attachment to a key family carer, and a very small number of other trustworthy, familiar adults. It really does seem that a template for future relationships rests on these early experiences. Young children cannot fend for themselves and their need for personal care should be met within a consistent experience of feeling nurtured. Their view of the social world is also shaped by whether important relationships are disrupted. Even the most resilient of children will eventually give up if familiar people, of whom they have become fond, disappear from daily life. Emotionally weary young children may resist getting acquainted with yet another unfamiliar person.

The initial approach to the significance of attachment in children's development started in the mid-1940s when John Bowlby studied a group of juvenile delinquents. Looking back into their personal histories, he found that many had experienced disruption in their early family attachments. Bowlby also documented the emotional distress of children who were evacuated from English cities in the early stage of the Second World War. Consistent with the prevailing theory of the time, Bowlby interpreted the emotional disruption in terms of the

children's loss of their mother. However, the evacuated children had been separated from other key family members; even siblings were sometimes allocated to different host families.

From the beginning, some child psychologists challenged Bowlby's interpretation of events. It is often unrecognised but, by the mid-1950s, Bowlby had moved from his original position that young children would suffer serious negative consequences if they were not continuously with their mother in particular. He was open to the importance of other key carers and the impact that separation from them could have on children. John Bowlby continued his research into the importance of early attachment, sometimes working with Mary Ainsworth, who explored ways to judge the strength of attachment between very young children and their mother from reactions to separation in an unfamiliar situation.

A resurgence of interest in attachment theory from the 1990s onwards has allowed for the reality that mothers are the important primary carer for many young children. However, the approach recognises that babies and children also develop strong attachments within their immediate family to their father, siblings and other relatives. Babies and young children tend to have a preferred familiar person, especially in times of upset or uncertainty. However, the young of the human species are

very social individuals under normal circumstances. The key factor for emotional security and psychologically healthy attachment is that other familiar adults, often family members, give sustained time and attention to get to know a baby or young child as an individual.

A greater understanding of how young children's brains develop has grown over the late 20th and early 21st centuries – much the same period when professionals involved with early years revisited the importance of attachment within early childhood. The human brain is highly responsive to events: the neural connections made within individual brain development are shaped by a child's experiences. What happens to children over early childhood really does matter. They build up an image of themselves, how they are treated and what they should expect in the future, especially of adults.

Even babies are working hard to make sense of their personal world. That task is made easier, and emotionally more supportive, when babies and young children recognise familiar ways of being treated. A small number of caring adults show that they believe it is worth their time to adjust to what makes this baby at ease, or dovetails with this child's interests and preferences. In contrast, fragmented and disrupted relationships mean that young children develop doubts about their own self worth. In a desperate bid for attention – any kind of attention – they often learn patterns of behaviour that bring further troubles.

The human brain works on electrical impulses plus chemicals and the balance within our body chemistry is directly affected by experiences. (You can read more about this area of research in Gerhardt 2004; Healy 2005; or Tayler 2007.) Cortisol, a steroid hormone, is important within the biochemistry of the brain. Human brains need cortisol; it is released in times of stress and helps the individual to focus on keeping safe and dealing with possible risks in an unfamiliar situation. Studies of cortisol levels have found that it tends to be raised when young children have to deal with a significant change in their familiar care arrangements. Examples have included starting at day nursery or the early weeks of primary school. The cortisol level tends to drop as young children feel more at ease. It is hard to be sure how much children feel emotional unease directly, and how much they are sensitive to the emotional distress of their parent. Parents are often uneasy or even upset when settling their toddler in a nursery or leaving a slightly older child at school. Even very young children recognise when a loved parent is not behaving normally and the child may mirror that anxiety or distress.

Cortisol levels are the internal chemical marker of what can be seen from the facial expression and other body language of a distressed child. All children will have times when they have to cope with change. Sensitive adult support – for instance through the key person approach – enables them to face future changes with a greater sense of confidence. However, young children whose early experiences are very unpredictable tend to have higher average levels of cortisol than peers whose life is emotionally more secure. The insecure and permanently alert young children are busy trying to work out what is happening today or how to get this person's attention. Without a secure and sustained relationship – in the family home or non-family provision – even very young children expect trouble and are constantly in a state of having to look out for themselves. Their pattern of behaviour makes warm relationships with adults or other children even more problematic.

Emotional wellbeing in early years provision

In past decades, young children in the UK rarely spent all their time as the sole responsibility of their mother until they started primary school. Children often spent some time with grandparents or experienced informal care from family friends. Increasingly, over-threes began to attend part-time provision, for instance in a nursery class or playgroup. However, from the 1990s onwards there was a significant increase in different kinds of non-family provision for under-fives. For some children this has meant shared care between home and nursery or childminder from the baby months. Other children have not experienced the transition until two or three years of age. This major social change for a generation of young children has meant that best practice has to consider children's need for attachment applied to non-family adults.

Research about young children's experiences in early years provision has provided a bewildering array of data. Until the 1970s it was largely assumed that children would be harmed by time spent in day nurseries, as out-of-home provision was viewed as inevitably disruptive of children's emotional attachment to their mothers. By the late 1970s several research reviews had challenged this stance, but still raised significant issues around the quality of children's experiences. A great deal depends on how young children are treated, wherever they spend their days. An unrealistic view that children will always be emotionally secure in their family life, for example, does not survive professional experiences of chaotic families and neglectful parents.

Practical observational research from the early 1980s homed in on the behaviour of adults, including choices about the organisation of day nurseries (see Bain and Barnett 1986; Hopkins 1988; or for an overview Lindon 2012a). The main issues continue to be very significant up to and including the current era. The main concern was that young children in groups could fail to be offered sufficient personal attention. Some practitioners seemed to feel it was not their job to be close to children, or were actively dissuaded by senior staff. Some practitioners struggled with their own feelings of distress, when they felt inadequate to meet the emotional needs of very young children. Some of these studies offered direct support to the practitioners in ways that have been repeated more recently (Croft 2009; Elfer et al. 2003).

Adults who felt more confident and competent were often better able to support young children with the nurture and emotional security they deserved. The approach we now call 'the key person' has evolved from these studies. Another significant source was the pioneering work of Elinor Goldschmied, who drew attention to the crucial, triangular relationship between the baby or child, the key person and the parent(s). She pointed out that a triangle is a stable shape, so long as each side is equally strong and each corner equally valued.

Responsible adults have to tackle the consequence of insecure attachment within early childhood because of the many problems that not acting can cause for the children later in life. The 1980s studies, and other anecdotal evidence that continues to this day, highlight two negative consequences of children growing up without secure attachments. Either pattern is observable in the behaviour of young children, when

they are emotionally adrift. A great deal depends on children's temperament, as well as the details of their experiences.

- Some young children give up trying to get close to adults, in this case early years practitioners, who appear to be emotionally unavailable and not to want the child physically close. These emotionally detached young children may then be classified as 'good' children, who are 'no trouble' and have 'settled-in well here', because the child does not cry or protest.

- An alternative, and broader pattern is that young children, even toddlers, learn to use strategies to ensure they receive attention. Since they are still very young, and adults ignore milder approaches, children's strategies risk becoming loud, physically aggressive, disruptive or regularly uncooperative. The second group of children, more than the first, were – and still are – likely to be labelled as 'behaviour problems'.

An additional point about attachment and behaviour has also arisen from more recent research about daycare starting as early as the baby year (overview in Lindon, 2012b). Some studies, not all, have raised concerns about increased patterns of aggressive behaviour and non-cooperation in children. Some commentators have reacted to this unwelcome finding as if it is an unprovoked attack on nurseries and working parents. Having read the research, I think this defensive reaction is unjustified. It is just as unprofessional now to reject any negative information about daycare, as it was in previous decades to insist that the impact must inevitably be detrimental to children.

In my view, careful consideration of older and more recent studies actually underlines the central importance of relationships for young children. Young children learn how to behave from being affectionately guided by familiar, caring adults. It seems very possible that more aggressive patterns of behaviour in some (but not all) young children, who have spent considerable time in daycare, could be explained by a lack of the close relationship which should be the essence of the key person role. In provision where practice is impersonal, young children have not been guided away from aggressive ways of dealing with the ordinary ups and downs of social interaction. As the months and then years roll by, older children remain stuck with the habits of a two-year-old in handling social dilemmas and actual disagreements.

The key person approach as normal practice

Young children need, and deserve, the same high quality of nurture and personal attention wherever they spend their days. The importance of those early experiences has led to considerable discussion around how to meet children's need for close relationships in different types of early years provision. There are two main practice questions:

- What is the nature of the relationship between adults who take significant, paid responsibility for young children, but who are not the child's parent or other family relative? This question applies equally to childminders, who mainly work alone, and to practitioners employed in group provision.

- How should this relationship be approached when there is more than one practitioner with whom a child could potentially relate? This question applies to group settings.

The revised EYFS (DfE, 2012) has confirmed that the key person approach is a non-negotiable requirement. In paragraph 1.11 the statutory framework states that each child must be assigned a key person; it is a safeguarding and welfare requirement. The childminding service shares the need to understand and discuss significant issues around close relationships with children and partnership with parents. The key person relationship is directly relevant to childminders. The organisational issues of a key person approach apply to early years group provision of all types.

The obligation to establish and maintain an effective key person approach is revisited in paragraph 3.26, as part of the revised welfare requirements. The role is that the key person should: 'help ensure that every child's care is tailored to meet their individual needs ... to help the child become familiar with the setting, offer a settled relationship for the child and build a relationship with their parents' (DfE, 2012, page 18).

Look closer: Garfield Children's Centre

The Garfield senior team have established a key person approach. They operate a co-working system: one named practitioner is the main key person and the other as the support. (This way of organising is also sometimes called partner key working or buddying.) The key person approach, and the focus on personal relationships, is fully established in the reception class, as well as the nursery.

The reception in Garfield has two classes, each led by a teacher, supported by an early years assistant. In each case, the reception class teacher fulfils the role of key person and their colleague is the co-key person. The consistent focus throughout the centre is on adults forming close relationships with children and their parents. The team's growing knowledge of individual children informs their flexible approach to planning, which leads through the current interests of three focus children each week.

Garfield reception class is part of the Children's Centre, which in turn is the early years section of Garfield Primary School. The nursery and reception teams both follow the same child-focused approach to observation and planning. It is a striking example of best practice that Garfield has successfully developed such a flexible approach within a reception class. It is so often a struggle to hold tight to best early years practice in this final year of the EYFS. The early years staff work as a consistent team with strong leadership, but they also have the full support of the primary school head.

A conscious choice was made to use the term 'key person' in the 2007 EYFS, and not 'key worker', which had been a common term. The revised EYFS remains true to this crucial, personal aspect. The approach is placed squarely with the necessity of building positive relationships with individual babies and children and their families. The statutory framework, in paragraph 1.11, states that early years providers have to inform parents or other family carers of the name of the child's key person. Part of the early relationship with a family is also explaining the role of the key person.

The revised EYFS continues to emphasise that the approach is not just for settling-in, nor is it an administrative role. The key person is the front line of the personalised approach for child and family.

The revised EYFS has strengthened the focus on partnership with parents, with this phrase in paragraph 1.11: 'The key person must seek to engage and support parents and/or carers in guiding their child's development at home. They should also help families engage with more specialist support if appropriate.' This emphasis is about partnership, not telling parents what to do in their own home, nor believing that all families need help (Lindon, 2009).

The role of the key person

- First and foremost, the key person is responsible for creating a personal relationship with the baby or child and his/her family. This relationship starts when it is clear that the parent(s) will take up a place in this provision.

- The key person is central to the beginning of the relationship, including the home visit, which is usual practice in many settings. She or he is also responsible for the settling in process – providing support for child and parent.

- Established practice in some settings is that the key person should now step back and ensure that the baby or child will 'go to anybody' in the room. However, this interpretation of a key person approach does not fit the definition in the EYFS. The key person approach is not exclusively for settling in; it is a relationship which lasts.

- It is appropriate and best practice that the key person continues to be the one who takes responsibility for the personal care of a baby or child. This named practitioner most usually greets key parents and children and has the personal conversation with individual parents at the end of the day. Alternatively the key person needs to ensure regular conversations with parents if this provision tends to end with a flurry of parents at much the same time.

- The key person takes responsibility for the records of their key children. But, this pattern coexists with the continued personal relationship. The key person approach does not become just an administrative role as soon as a child is judged to be settled.

The key person approach applies across early childhood. It is not something that can be sidelined for the over-threes and it continues to apply as a legal obligation for reception classes, the final year of the EYFS.

I have encountered reception classes (see the Garfield Children's case study on page 5) who have established a proper key person system. In my experience, those reception teams who fulfil this legal obligation are fully supported by the head of the primary school where they are based. They are given a secure and more appropriate ratio than the bare minimum of one adult to every 30 children, which has been confirmed in the revised EYFS on paragraph 3.37. This unworkable ratio remains a significantly negative feature of the EYFS, since it treats children younger than statutory education age as if they are already pupils in a school classroom.

Some early years settings have a long established key person approach that operates in the way envisaged by the EYFS. Other settings, with children younger than five, have run a system in which the named key practitioner has a time-limited role and children are soon expected to relate to any member of staff.

The move to a sustained, personal approach with young children poses a significant change for some groups, including the need to address the reasons that previously seemed to justify a more impersonal system. However, practitioners who are experienced at working with a genuine key person approach still recognise that details need to be revisited and any concerns fully aired.

The key person approach in practice

The statutory requirement, plus the related EYFS guidance, is very clear. Early years practitioners should develop a continuing, personal relationship with individual babies and children, and their family. In any kind of group provision, this relationship can only be achieved through organising a key person system. In the childminding service, practitioners should also take a key person approach, with the difference that the most usual situation is that childminders work alone in their own family home. In much of what follows, 'key person' has to be read as the named practitioner in a group and a childminder in her or his own home.

Building a relationship with families

Young children need to spend enough time within their own family so that their emotional attachment is secure and their parents feel confident about dealing with their behaviour. However, a close relationship needs to be nurtured between practitioner and parent(s): a pattern of genuinely shared care and shared affection for a baby or young child. Otherwise, young children are emotionally adrift between two social worlds.

- Parents need to feel confident that this key person notices and cherishes their baby or child. But young children benefit also from seeing their important familiar adults in a communicative, friendly relationship. They feel that parts of their daily life are connected and children know that parents and their key person appear comfortable with each other.

- Friendly adult-to-adult communication is the way that you hear what this family would prefer. There are many choices that arise over early childhood, because there are diverse ways to raise happy, healthy babies and children. Practitioners need to feel that their role is valued as well. Partnership does not mean agreeing to everything a parent requests, without reference to a child's wellbeing or the core values of the nursery or childminding service.

- With a key person approach, you are likely to be told by a parent about happy and interesting family events that young children struggle to share, until they have the words. A friendly working relationship with parents also makes it likely they will trust you with sensitive information about family events or upheavals that will affect the child.

The story of your close relationship with a baby or child and the family starts with the conversational meeting when parents have

Links to your practice

Your relationship with a family has a life that starts with parents' first impressions when they contact your setting, or you as an individual childminder, to enquire about what you offer. Every enquiry does not turn into a request for a place. However, those first impressions are important, even for parents who decide not to follow up their contact.

Many neighbourhoods have a busy local grapevine and positive reactions will travel from parents who have not joined your provision: "Lovely nursery (or childminder), but in the end I chose somewhere closer to my work". Negative reactions will also travel: "The manager (or childminder) just talked about meeting all these regulations; she didn't seem interested in me or my son".

decided they will accept the offer of a place in your setting, or home as a childminder. The aims of this first meeting are to set the right tone for the friendly working relationship that will follow. Your aim is always to work in partnership with parents or other family members closely involved with this baby or child. The nature of this relationship and other aspects of partnership are discussed in detail in Lindon (2012).

Many group settings offer a home visit to families. The named key person, often with a colleague, goes to the family home, with the aim of having the first lengthy conversation in a setting that is comfortable for the parent(s). The advantage is also that toddlers and young children first meet their future key person in familiar surroundings. It is not unusual for slightly older children to recall this first time once they are in their nursery and say: "You saw my bedroom and my Teddy". In the childminding service the usual pattern would be to invite the parent(s) and child to visit the childminder's own home.

You need to steadily gather information about the family, as well as ensure that parents have heard and understand the conditions and boundaries to the place that is offered by this setting, or within your childminding service. However, it is unwise to try to cover everything in one marathon sitting. Fellow adults do not take in a considerable amount of information in one go, especially if some concepts or words are unfamiliar, even to parents who share the same fluent language as you. Be ready to revisit, repeat and rephrase ideas or the boundaries to what you offer to any family, or the specialist package offered to this family.

Within the early part of your relationship with the family you need to cover knowledge about family cultural background, faith if any, and home language(s) as a necessary basis for you to understand family life. Be alert to areas in which you need to check; whether this is about diet, family naming systems, or anything that could affect daily life with this child and parent(s). A good rule of thumb is that if in doubt, you ask. Certainly avoid any assumption that a social group label is a quick and easy way to know how this individual family operates day by day. There is a considerable amount of variation within any cultural, ethnic or faith group and some family choices are precisely that – what this individual family prefers to do. (See Lindon 2012c for more about best practice in equality.)

Information about individual children enables a secure beginning for a relationship between the key person and this baby or child. In group provision, the key person is responsible for sharing that knowledge with colleagues, especially the buddy/partner key person for this family.

- Personal details matter, such as how this child is known within the family – for instance by a shortened version of their full name or by their second rather than first personal name. If Natasha is always called Tasha at home, she will not respond if addressed by the wrong name. If she is always known as Natasha, it is not alright for her key person or anyone else to shorten it to Tash. If a name is unfamiliar to you, then ensure that parents help you to say it properly, as well as get the correct spelling on any written records.

Links to your practice

You will of course, continue to learn about this child's immediate or extended family. But from the beginning the key person should be aware of siblings or other relatives who are part of the immediate family.

Many teams and individual childminders ask families if they could provide a family photo, as well as an individual photo of the child. The family photo may be laminated, so that it will last in the child's personal basket or drawer. As well as personal items, a photo can be an important link with home that children can literally hold in their hands. A photo of the baby or child will usually start the individual portfolio/folder that will grow over time to document this personal learning journey.

Links to your practice

In full-day nurseries, some babies or young children have a longer day in the setting than any practitioner. In this context the key person approach is sometimes organised by partner key working, sometimes called 'buddying'. Individual children with their family have a named key person with a known back-up person from the team.

- Family living arrangements are diverse and within early meetings with the family, ideally within the home visit, you will hear how life works for this child. Your relationship is then based on an accurate understanding. Perhaps one parent travels a great deal for work and missing Daddy – or Mummy – is a regular event for this child. If some or most of the families attending your provision are part of the armed services, then absence and an underlying concern about safety will be part of family life.

- Family structure can vary when babies or children live with their birth parent(s). It is professional – not being nosy – to understand this child's family organisation: who is the primary carer, do two parents share the care over the week, is there a system of co-parenting across two households? Some children may be in the permanent care of another relative, such as their grandparents.

- Some children are not with their birth family – either on a temporary or a permanent basis. They may be with foster carers or have been adopted by the parents you meet. You need to be told how a child names their foster carers or, in a less usual situation for under-fives, their key person from a residential children's home. Any family should be reassured that private details will be kept confidential, with the proviso that you explain – early in the relationship – your professional obligation over safeguarding.

Those early meetings establish the base that a key person can be trusted. You want to make connections between home and non-family time. It will help when you can name the people in photos that matter to this child.

If you are a key person to a baby or young toddler, you need to learn about that individual from the parent(s). Your aim is to provide as much continuity as possible with existing personal routines and to understand the current position for any family on changes like weaning or toilet training. But the key person also needs to know the personal version for this baby or child. The fact that you ask, and listen, to how ordinary routines work in family life is reassuring to parents: you want to know what is usual for their baby or child.

- Is the baby breast-fed and will her mother want to arrange to visit the nursery or your home as a childminder to continue breastfeeding? If the mother wishes to express breast milk, has her baby accepted familiar milk provided in an initially unfamiliar bottle?

- How does six-month-old Teja show hunger, thirst or tiredness? How does she currently like to be fed, winded, comforted into or out of sleep? How does seventeen-month-old Yinka show he is tired and how does he currently sleep in the day or have a regular restful time?

- Do young toddlers have personal words or gestures that indicate how they feel? Do they have an important comfort object or cuddly, that will need to accompany them into the nursery or childminder's home? Do they have a favourite song, game or book?

- How does two-year-old Simon indicate he needs to use the potty? Does two-year-old Alicia prefer sitting on the toilet with a child insert seat? Unless there is a very good reason, you would usually continue the routine that this child knows.

- The key person needs to understand those important little things that will make a big difference to this individual baby or child. Alicia may be able to talk, yet not be able to tell you that she likes custard, but only on the side of her pudding, never, ever over the top.

- You need to know this child's main medical history, including any special needs – whether an allergy, chronic health condition, diet or disability. Partnership with parents will be your route to understand how this individual child lives with a given level of a specific disability. Even practitioners with

experience of a given chronic health condition cannot know at the outset what it means for this individual child day by day.

Look closer: Kennet Day Nursery

The team are active in finding ways to build the bridge between home and nursery. During the early part of getting to know a child and family, the key person is alert to learn about a child's current interests, through conversation with parents, as well as what children themselves show or say.

During my visit to Kennet, Abi, nearly two-years-old, was on his second full day at nursery. His key person already knew from conversation with his mother that Abi was keen on music and singing. He also enjoyed wielding the vacuum cleaner at home. Abi's key person had made sure that the musical instruments and toys were easily visible, as was the child-size vacuum cleaner. She was also ready to respond to any request from Abi about singing.

Children need a period of careful settling into your home or the setting. The pattern of this supportive process will not be identical across provision. However, common features should be that it is a period of time and not a one-off event, immediately followed by the full version of the place that has been offered to this family. Childminders need to explain how they want to work together with parents to ease a child into what is currently an unfamiliar place. In group provision the key person should be able to explain the broad policy for settling in and there should be a consistent approach across any group setting. This aspect of beginning the relationship is explained in a personal way to parents when it becomes clear that this family will join your provision.

There will be flexibility for a personalised approach for individual babies and children. However, the process of settling in should not be curtailed because a family wants it to be fast. Key persons in nurseries and childminders need to understand the pressures on working parents, or the problems for students when their childcare arrangements have been finalised too close to the beginning of their course of study. But your prime responsibility has to be the emotional wellbeing of this baby or child and a secure start to your relationship with them, not the unfamiliar figure in whose arms they are left with minimal warning.

You need a clear agreement about a series of visits when the parent will stay with their baby and child and how the length of that visit steadily increases. There will not be an inflexible pattern, but it is likely to be at least three-four separate visits. Some settings make it clear to the family that someone will need to be available for a given period of time, for instance, over an agreed fortnight. It is appropriate to be flexible to the family in terms of who will take responsibility for the settling-in process (see page 8 about different family structures). The aim of a settling-in process is to support the separation for the baby or child from the adult they know best. So the process is also about supporting and reassuring that adult.

In a group setting, the key person should definitely be present on each of these settling-in visits, and will be responsible for introducing the parent to the partner key person and other team members. It would not be appropriate for the key person to be absent, for training or a holiday, over the settling-in period. It does not matter how well the home visit or other early conversations appear to have gone. In the future, you should let your key parents know if you will be away. In full year provision practitioners will take holidays at some point and the senior team needs to ensure that a key person and back up are not away at the same time.

Look closer: Kennet Day Nursery

At the time of the home visit, the Kennet team provide the reassuring "A parent's guide to settling into nursery", which consists of a short explanation including tips about settling a baby or child into nursery. Expressed in my own words, these are some of the key points of the guide:

■ **Of course children are keen to stay close to their parent in an unfamiliar situation. There is no rush. Children vary over how long they need to become at ease.**

■ **Parents will help best by, over several short visits, gradually allowing a little more physical distance between themselves and their child. A suggestion is for parents to be ready to show an interest in a book or other resource in another part of the room or chat with another adult.**

■ **Children can then explore and establish the beginnings of a close relationship with their key person and notice other children too. Their parent is still present and easily available.**

■ **Babies and young children take their cue from familiar adults. If their parent looks happy and relaxed in this new place, then their baby or child is likely to think this experience could be alright.**

■ **Parents are definitely advised to say a proper goodbye and not just to disappear when the child is distracted. This separation can begin with parents saying they will be gone for only a few minutes, and then leaving the room and returning very soon. The time can be steadily increased until the parent does leave for the first stretch of time, building up to the full amount of time that this baby or child will be with the nursery under usual circumstances.**

During the settling-in process, the key person's role is to support the parent, or other family carer, to ease back a little from their son or daughter, as the child becomes more at ease with you.

■ This process is slow and steady and the key person needs to be ready to reassure the parent that this process is not a race; it is irrelevant how easily, or not, other babies or young children have settled in the past. If necessary, let this parent know that it is very usual for older babies and young children to want to remain close to their parent in a currently unfamiliar situation.

- Even children who are already familiar with your provision, because they have accompanied a parent to pick up an older sibling, still need and deserve the settling-in process. Your careful judgement, in partnership with the parent, may be that three-year-old Becky looks only too pleased finally to have full access to what up to now was her three older siblings' playgroup. She may need less time to be fully at ease here. The focus of settling in is also on the parent: maybe Becky's mother looks downcast at being waved away in a cheery fashion by her youngest child.

- However, it can also happen that two-year-old Freddy initially looks very pleased with his new nursery. Then it becomes clear that, unlike Stay-and-Play sessions, his Daddy is going to leave – an unexpected and unwelcome turn of events for Freddy. It will make a difference if Freddy's key person already knows about his prior experiences in any kind of early years provision or flexible drop-in sessions.

- Perhaps Angie's mother says her daughter will settle quickly because she has attended several different childminders or groups. This information is not necessarily a positive omen. Angie may well have experienced too many changes and be less than happy about yet another new place and people.

A personal relationship with children

Overall, the key person approach is needed for the wellbeing of young children. Understood and organised appropriately, the approach complements the strong, much longer relationship that children have with their own parents and family. Young children do not have a finite bag of affection. A sustained, affectionate relationship with their key person does not reduce the affection available for parents. It is also true that young children need to spend enough time with their own parent(s), to build strong emotional bonds and a shared history of happy memories.

Part of your close relationship with children is that you ease those regular transition times when they pass from the responsibility of one person to another. The beginning and end of the day or session are also that time when communication between the key person and the parent builds the bridge between the family home and the nursery or home of a childminder. Simple and regular conversation is the main route of communication. But this contact will be supported by a home-provision sheet or daily diary, especially for the personal care of babies and toddlers. Parents need to know simple highlights of their child's day: what has held a child's attention, or what was special about their time in the sand this afternoon. You show at this time that you are equally interested to hear about family life. You welcome any

anecdotes and photos travelling into your provision as well as in the direction from you to home.

From the home visit, and certainly by the end of the settling-in period, you should be clear who will be the main family member, and the one or two other trusted adults, who will bring and pick up this baby or child.

Links to your practice

Key persons working in sessional provision need to understand a family's pattern of childcare that fits around less than full day provision. You need to meet and get to know other early years practitioners who are closely involved in this child's daily life. In some cases it will be a childminder or nanny who usually drops the child off and picks the child up from your provision.

However, it is still definitely preferable that a parent is the person involved in settling-in their child. This process is also the beginning of your partnership with the parent(s), or the key family carer, like a grandparent. Future communication may sometimes have to be through another named and trusted person and you need a good working relationship with them. However, if you do not establish a personal relationship with the parent at settling in, it will be difficult to create effective communication in the future about the development and wellbeing of their child.

Links to your practice

Parents who choose the childminding service will have one person, at most two, to get to know and recognise. On the other hand, even in a relatively small nursery, parents will see quite a few faces in addition to the key person and partner, who will become familiar from the early days. Adults vary as to how well they recognise faces of other people they have met before.

It is quite usual for nurseries and other group provision to have a board with photos of everyone in the team, including roles like the cook or a gardener. Perhaps you could gather these images on a single sheet and give a copy to parents new to the setting. In a large centre, you might restrict it to the team that covers the age range of this child. You could circle the key person for this family.

Some settings print a sheet explaining how the key person system works. Another possibility, that I have encountered is to set this up so you can personalise each sheet by inserting a photo of the individual practitioner who is the key person for this family.

The key person, in group provision that is less than full day, may pass a child into the responsibility of a childminder, a nanny or a practitioner from an extended day service. You need to know the predictable pattern, so that you can reassure the child and guide their expectations day by day in a variable week.

Some early years provision has to discuss with families how old a sibling needs to be to take this responsibility. A childminder has to resolve any difference of opinion with the parent(s). In group provision, key persons need to be sure of the setting's policy, so they do not appear to be making a random personal decision that two-year-old Greg cannot be passed into the sole charge of his nine-year-old sister.

The family also needs to let you know if there is anyone who definitely should not be allowed to take the child. In families with a history of domestic violence a father or mother may definitely not be safe alone with their baby or child. A similar situation may arise in unresolved custody disputes where there is a risk that a disaffected parent may take the child and disappear. Key persons, supported by their senior staff in a group setting, need to be fully informed about this kind of situation and have the professional responsibility to ask for explanations. You cannot safeguard a child without sufficient information.

Children and parents are all individuals, so there is no set pattern for how to ease the daily separation, once the settling-in period is complete.

Links to your practice

A quiet corner may be the best for parent and child to enable a peaceful transfer. You need to be available as a key person for individual babies or children to choose to transfer into close contact with you, sometimes directly into your arms. The time will come when a toddler or child arrives and heads straight to their preferred resources or friends. You can then have a personal, maybe brief chat, with the parent.

Even children who have settled into your provision can have times when they are distressed by the separation. The best approaches to ease the transfer, but accept that when a parent has to leave the child may well cry and protest. You do not try to jolly them out of this distress. You recognise with words and body language "you're sad today" or "you found it hard to wave goodbye to Daddy this morning". You welcome children to stay by you and do not rush them into activities in an attempt to distract them from their feelings.

The crucial point underpinning all this support is that early years practitioners are comfortable with touch, physical closeness to young children and cuddling them. All the settings I visited for this book shared this best practice approach.

Children are unsettled by an abrupt departure or lack of any proper goodbye from their parent or other family carer. It is wise to explain, if necessary, that parents should not just disappear when the child's attention is elsewhere.

You need to have a sensitive conversation with any parents whose own unease becomes a very long drawn out goodbye, giving the impression that they almost want the child to be distressed before they leave.

It would be unprofessional for a key person to sit in critical judgement on parents who mishandle the separation or handover. You help a baby or child by trying to understand the feelings of a parent, who may be in two minds about leaving. However, you need also to keep your attention equally on the wellbeing of individual babies or children.

Some parents may need reassurance that their child does not forget them. Real examples will help: how a child recalls or talks about parents and family events during the day, maybe looking at the family photo(s) in a personal basket.

In a way that is sensitive to individual parents, the key person needs to let mothers or fathers know that their toddler missed them or was excited to see them come in the door – despite the fact that this delight is now being expressed by loud shouts and running round in circles.

As the key person, you have to achieve a delicate balance between honesty that a child takes a little while to be happy after separation and worrying a parent that their baby or child is distressed for a long time. You undoubtedly face a tough decision, if the weeks pass and a child remains hard to console.

If there is a choice, parents may be best supported to consider delaying the child's entry into your sessional playgroup until some months have passed. Some young twos are not ready for a busy group setting and a generation ago we would not have thought there was any developmental problem with their refusal to settle. However, the senior team needs to be sure that the learning environment and practitioners' expectations are developmentally appropriate for very young children.

The key person needs to be confident that recognition and acceptance of children's feelings is crucial. The measure of a 'good' practitioner is not that you can stop children crying quickly. Best practice is that the child feels and looks emotionally safe with you and they stop crying in their own time. In a group setting it is important (and discussed further on page 32) that practitioners have easy opportunities to talk with the senior team or with experienced room colleagues. The measure of good team working is that colleagues do not get tetchy when a key person dedicates time to comforting a distressed child. They see you are fully occupied and do their best to give you and the child the peace that is needed.

The description of the statutory key person approach (see page 5) focuses on nurture. The only sensible interpretation of that paragraph is that the key person does most of the personal care and is easily available when key children are going through a tough time emotionally.

■ The key person, or their back-up in partner key working, attends to this child's physical needs. The key person approach should operate within routines that are flexible to the needs of individual babies and toddlers. So the key person changes the nappy of a baby or toddler when that child needs changing. Very young children need to become familiar with the voice and face of the person who changes and feeds them, or to whom they wake from a nap.

■ The key person should be responsible for completing the daily records that are part of good care of babies and very young children: documenting their sleep and eating patterns, nappy changes and toilet training when that becomes relevant.

■ It is usual that this record, often in a diary format, is given to the parent at the end of day and brought back the following day, or whichever is the child's next time in nursery or with the childminder.

■ Parents are welcome to add to the record as their contribution to keeping the channels of communication

fully open, when a baby or child cannot contribute to the understanding of 'what happened today'.

■ This record should also include a highlight or two of the day: not a bland description of what he or she did but a feel of why the child's time in the sand was special or some element of "what I'd tell you if I had the words" (with thanks to Staffordshire University Nursery where I first saw this phrase).

■ The key person really gets to know an individual baby or toddler. The adult then understands the child's preferences and develops personal rituals of songs, smiles and enjoyable 'jokes'.

The key person sometimes has to reach a compromise with parents' wishes. Mild or more significant differences of opinion may arise over weaning, the timing of toilet training or patterns of rest and sleep. Partnership means listening to and understanding what a parent has asked. It does not mean agreeing to everything that is requested. For instance, perhaps Tasha's mother is firm that she does not want her daughter to take an afternoon nap anymore. Tasha's key person agrees to try. However, the pattern is that Tasha is irritated and exhausted by mid-afternoon. Unless constantly watched, she finds a cosy corner and is out like a light. Tasha's key person can express sympathy for the mother's wish not to have her daughter awake into the evening. However, the key person has to have a sensitive conversation based on the consequences for the child of taking away her nap at the moment.

Look closer: Kennet Day Nursery
Individual routines in the nursery are kept very personal. The care and a nurturing environment are highly valued in this setting.

1) During one day in my visits, Jamie, an older toddler, woke from his nap and his key person made it easy for him to take his time to be ready to get up fully. Jamie looked around the room and his key person responded to his look and gestures. Jamie was interested to communicate that the baby was no longer in her cot, as she had been when he fell asleep for his nap. Jamie then looked around the room at the young children who were awake and playing. His key person followed his gaze and interest, naming each child as Jamie pointed to them and looked expectantly at her. Jamie pulled at his socks and again his key person followed that visual sign with "yes, there's your stripy socks".

2) At another point in my visit I was sitting by Harry, aged two-and-a-half, who had been very busy with stickle bricks for at least ten minutes. He had built a number of small structures on his base and experimented with joining pieces together, which he described as a sword. His key person explained courteously to Harry that she needed to check if his nappy needed to be changed, and it did. She offered to carry his construction on the base and Harry took two fistfuls of smaller stickle bricks.

Harry was happy to be changed, his key person had placed his construction in full view and Harry continued to hold onto some bricks. When he was fully changed, Harry's key person came with him back to the table with the stickle bricks, set the construction back on the table and waited to see if Harry needed any support. However, Harry went straight back to his construction, with the same level of concentration as before, and continued to construct different items for about another ten minutes.

Harry's key person explained to me that he was not always very keen to have his nappy changed but was at ease if he could bring something with him. Her approach also ensured that the nappy change did not bring Harry's chosen play to an end. It was striking that his key person's sensitive approach had enabled this very young child to get back to his project of interest and enjoy a sustained period of concentration.

Penny Tassoni (2008) points out that, when the key person approach is working well, it should not be difficult for an observant visitor to identify a child's key person with a fair degree of accuracy. In a group setting, it should be the key person who undertakes the personal care of a baby or child. But also, key children often touch base with their key person at regular intervals – either glancing over or wanting this special adult to look or listen to something important. It is likely to be this person to whom a child turns when a bit upset, tired or unwell. They are not being 'clingy'; they are

being young children and it is reassuring for a visiting consultant to see them gathered affectionately.

As a visitor to settings with a genuine key person approach, I find that practitioners have no difficulty in telling me the back story to what their key children are enthused about today. You can read one example below and more in Lindon (2010). The key person knows the continuing narrative about their key children's learning and is visibly interested and excited about their children's current and next steps in the learning journey. They have a professionally appropriate pride in the children and share with parents in a way that makes connections between nursery and home.

Look closer: Kennet Day Nursery
I could see a display on one of the walls in Kingfishers (the three-to-fives room), which included a child's name and other mark making. I was told the learning story that led up to this display. Three weeks ago Tony's key person and her colleagues had noticed that Tony (3yrs, 5mths) was very interested in the set of pebbles with letters on them. He was choosing to organise the pebbles and looked carefully at them. So they decided to put out the letter mats with Tony in mind, but not exclusively for him. Tony was very interested and spent time lining up the mats and looking with care.

Another day Tony was absorbed in a junk modelling activity and went to collect the letter pebbles, his name card and, out of his own choice, decided to write his name. His key person admired his work (as a visitor, I could see it was recognisably his name) and asked if it would be alright to put the writing onto the room display board. Tony said that would be fine, he would make another one for his Mummy, which he did. Tony took an active part in making his part of the display, creating further mark marking with paper plates and deciding how the different parts of his work should be fixed onto the board.

In all the settings visited for this book the key person took responsibility for the personal records of their key children. This best practice means that someone has clear responsibility for keeping a child's daily records and their developmental learning journey fully up-to-date. In all the teams the pattern was definitely that the key person welcomed insights and observations from colleagues. It would not be good practice to have any sense of possessiveness over 'my children – my records'. However, it can become confused if the pattern is that any practitioner in the room can make entries in any record. Key persons should know individuals really well, so they can make connections and promote child-initiated learning (Lindon, 2010) with flexible short-term plans responsive to children's current interests.

Look closer: Randolph Beresford Early Years Centre

In this setting the key person takes responsibility for regular contributions to their key children's personal folder.

Continued professional support is available for ensuring that descriptions are informative and any photos are chosen for a reason that rests on the significance of that experience for a child. The key person can also include a sketch or other helpful visual. I looked at one folder in which the practitioner had drawn the climbing equipment to show the route that had been achieved in a significant clamber that this young child had chosen to do.

The key person also considers this individual child's learning priorities on the basis of current development and interests. A personalised approach to planning rests on this knowledge. In each team meeting it is possible to raise 'a child of concern' – the way this team describe an individual who, for whatever reason, is on the minds of the key person or room colleagues.

The explicit policy of the RBEYC senior team is that practitioners have to be trusted: that key persons will always have personal knowledge of children in their head. It is unnecessary to require excessive amounts of writing down information. The team values anecdotal conversations about individual children and further thoughts about key children can emerge in this informal way.

Key person times

In a group setting, practitioners are not by the side of their key children throughout every moment of the session or day. Even toddlers and very young children become confident enough that they move around what is now a familiar environment. They choose to make contact with other individual adults and with children who become their favourite play companions. The key person remains important, but does not carry the entire responsibility for the emotional wellbeing of their key children. That responsibility is shared with the child's own family and shared appropriately with colleagues. The key person remains central to their key children. They have a special, close relationship, supported by the fact that they spend regular time together – often for lunch but also for regular key group time.

Look closer: Kennet Day Nursery

The nursery team aim to provide a friendly and predictable pattern to the day, valuing routines for children and not creating an inflexible schedule. The children have a rolling snack time, in which they join the snack table when they are ready to take a break in their play. There is always an adult at the table to keep children company and offer any help. Toddlers and children do not have to stop their chosen activity for a set snack time. They have a chance to enjoy their drink and snack at a time that suits them.

Lunchtimes are a sit down, social occasion when children usually sit in their key groups, but are welcome to shift if they want to sit with a friend. Children help as much as possible

for their age and personal ability. By the time children join Kingfishers at about three years of age they are able to be active in the lunchtime routine. Some children take responsibility each day for laying the tables, including the individual photo place mats for each child. They bring the food in serving dishes from the serving table, where the lunch has arrived from the kitchen in heatproof containers.

Conversation flowed over the lunch. One group was busy recalling what happened this morning and another key group was deep into hearing about one child's family visit to a farm. Children ate their lunch and chatted, and were active in helping themselves and each other. Children take responsibility for tidying up their own plate and cutlery to the trolley – a routine that a four-year-old boy explained clearly and courteously to me, as a visitor.

The idea of key group time was developed by Elinor Goldschmied, as part of her child-focused approach to secure relationships within the nursery environment (Goldschmied and Jackson, 2004). She called this time 'the island of intimacy' and suggested that a suitable timing could be just before lunch in full day nurseries. Key person time is a protected event that happens in a regular predictable time slot every day.

The content of this special shared time needs to be flexible and is certainly not a highly structured, adult organised, pre-planned time. It is an enjoyable shared time and contributes to the flexible planning informed by young children's interests that is a cornerstone of best early years practice as outlined in the EYFS. I have seen and heard of key groups who go on visits to other areas in a large centre. Examples have been under-threes who enjoyed the big children's garden while the over-threes were busy laying tables for their own lunch, or going to say hello to adults in the office or to see, with great interest, other parts of a large building in which the nursery is located. Two detailed examples are given below.

Look closer: Start Point Sholing Early Years Centre

In the nursery class at Start Point Sholing, the three- and four-year-olds come together in key groups for about 20-25 minutes mid-morning and mid-afternoon. They spend time with their key person, and sometimes an additional adult, focused on an activity that the practitioner knows is of direct interest to them.

On the day of my visit some key groups went outside. I stayed with the group of five children who were keen to create a story using dolls that could hook onto a finger and some wooden items. The practitioner supported the group with open-ended questions: "What's our story going to be called?" and the agreement was "the princess and the queen and the fairies and the pea". Then she guided with questions like: "How's our story going to start?" and "what's going to happen next?". The narrative grew and the practitioner wrote each part onto her clipboard as the children agreed upon the details. All the children were active in developing the interlocking story lines: starting with the princess who "got soggy and wet in the rain and the storm", some horses that appeared and the fairies who were ready to save everyone.

Once this story was complete, to the children's satisfaction, their key person read it back to them and they acted out the narrative scene by scene. Three children wanted to leave and play elsewhere, which was fine, and two children were keen to develop a second story, entitled The Bread in the Bed. This narrative featured ghosts and the bread, which had a life of its own. Again, the practitioner helped to develop the story, but firmly based on what the children determined. So, when it was announced by one child that: "The ghost is in the bath", she asked: "What's he doing in there?" and the reply was "he's washing his hair". As the story seemed to reach an uncertain conclusion, the adult asked for clarity: "What happens to the ghost?" and then "what about the bread?". In fact, everyone was dead and that definitely was the end.

Stories like this are written up by the practitioner in Start Point Sholing, so children have access to what they have created.

Look closer: Ladybirds Pre-School:

Ladybirds has a scheduled 20 minute key person time relatively early within the separate morning and afternoon sessions. The focus of this time is decided on the basis of children's current interests and remains flexible to what catches their interests today.

I followed one key group who went outside to investigate the current development of individual tadpoles. At the time of my visit, Ladybirds Pre-School had a large deep container with tadpoles who were on their way towards turning into frogs. Some children had taken home a tadpole over the Easter holiday break and family stories about tadpoles were being gathered.

One girl and her father had chosen to keep a tadpole diary over the holiday and this account had already been laminated and placed within the tadpole area, which was also set up with some books about frogs. On the day of my visit, another child had brought back his tadpole, together with a story written with his family about what had happened over the holiday. The boy carefully poured the tadpole back into the main container. The practitioner enabled the boy to share his story, which included how interested his cat had been in the tadpole. The family had been concerned, but the cat had just tried to drink the water in the bowl and not to gobble the tadpole. This story was also to be laminated and placed in the area.

The children were fascinated and wanted to talk about the tadpoles. They also used magnifying glasses which had been left in this area. The practitioner followed the conversation that the children wanted to have today. They were all looking closely at the tadpoles and the adult reflected on some of the children's comments with suggestions such as: "How do they move?", and one child replied and pointed, "with their tails". Children spontaneously commented on the development of individual tadpoles with "it's bigger than that one", "that one's sinking down" and gave some tadpoles names.

The practitioner had a camera and offered for children to take photos if they wished. At this point one child called everyone's attention to a loud noise out on the road. It was the refuse collectors in their truck. One key group – adult and children – headed across the garden to get a better look at the refuse truck and what was going on. They watched until the truck moved on and a child encouraged the practitioner with "take a picture", which she did.

The continued, close relationship between the key person, the children and their families is the channel through which parents are able to share important highlights of their child's day and their learning journey over those hours that the parent does not directly see and hear.

Best practice over the key person approach is closely connected with equally good practice over personalised key group times and flexible planning that is highly responsive to children's current interests. These examples, from two of the settings I visited for this book, give you an excellent flavour of what works in the best interests of children.

Look closer: Making Rice Krispies® cakes in Kennet Day Nursery

In this setting the three- and four-year-olds come together at the end of the morning for key group time, in which they share an experience – indoors or outdoors – with their key person and other children in the key group. The activity at this time of the day is adult-initiated and, as appropriate to the activity, sometimes adult-led. The content of these key group times is planned ahead but written guiding plans usually stretch no more than two weeks ahead.

I sat with one key group of four children, their key person and a second practitioner as they implemented their plan for today which was to follow the recipe for making chocolate Rice Krispies cakes. This activity was a relaxed experience lasting around 30 minutes and the practitioner kept the children fully involved from the outset when he started with "what do we need?" and took the ingredients out of the shopping bag one by one. The query "what's the first thing we need to do?" was understood by all the children to be that they washed their hands before starting to cook. They went and fetched their own bowls from where they are stored

and organised their own set of paper cases. The cooking table buzzed with conversation, both from the children initiating questions and comments and the adult guiding them through the recipe.

Children broke up segments of chocolate into their individual bowl and considered the adult's question of whether the chocolate would mix in its current state. The children were clear about 'no' and then listened as the adult suggested: "We could get it hot and then it will m..." waiting for a child to guess 'melt'. The cooking conversation continued with his asking: "How could we make it melt?" and the group considered several possibilities. With hints from their key person, the group agreed that they could use the microwave, which was located in the kitchen area.

The practitioner took one child at a time, with their bowl of chocolate and guided the child over putting the bowl into the microwave, pressing the correct buttons for time, waiting and then taking the bowl out. The children were able to do this sequence with the guidance of their key person and added to their existing skills of how to be safe in an ordinary kitchen.

Each child returned to the table and set about mixing in Rice Krispies with their now melted chocolate. Each child had their own copy of the recipe sheet, with the four written steps and pictures. The second practitioner remained sitting at the table and was part of the conversation that continued to flow.

Both practitioners modelled checking the steps of the recipe by words and visuals and reviewed the steps with any child who wanted. By the end of the activity a considerable number of chocolate Rice Krispies had been completed. The aim was to make enough for other children to share at teatime today.

Over this relaxed time, children continued to chat and make choices about what interested them.

■ One girl (3yrs, 5mths), focusing on the letters on the large packet of Rice Krispies, believed that the 'e' was the letter for 'Mummy'. The adult swiftly realised that the confusion arose because her mother's personal name began with the letter 'e'. The practitioner gave a simple explanation that acknowledged this was a sensible mistake and together they looked for, and found, an 'm' for Mummy.

■ Another child of a similar age decided to count the number of cakes in the tray and she lost track at one point. The key person simply looked doubtful and suggested that maybe she could try again. She looked with care and counted just the filled cases and then invited by the practitioner, realised she had not counted her own two.

■ Another child spotted other recipes on the back of the packet and a discussion followed about which recipes they would do on another day. The key person confirmed that the chosen recipe would definitely be the plan and they would just need to work out what ingredients needed to be bought.

When the children had made all the cakes to their own satisfaction, they helped with wiping the table and tidying up and placed their recipe sheet in their personal drawer.

In Kennet Day Nursery, the plans are definitely open to being changed in response to children's expressed interests, right up to and including at the time. During the morning that I watched, a different key group had started with a shared book. The children had become increasingly interested in the Rice Krispies cakes being made on the next table and their key person responded swiftly to their obvious interest. She checked whether there were sufficient ingredients for her group to get cooking and, when the answer was yes, she and the children reorganised themselves.

There was a back story to the key group time that I enjoyed observing. The key person to this group of three- and four-year-olds explained that what I had seen was only the latest in a range of experiences around cooking, since the group included some keen cooks. In the previous autumn, when some of this key group were just three-years-old, he had noticed that two boys spent a lot of time pretend cooking with the play dough. He decided to organise a trip to a nearby pizza restaurant, which welcomed school groups to visit, including a behind the scenes tour.

The restaurant manager was doubtful that such young children would get much out of a visit but agreed. The children were fascinated by their tour, asked questions, made their pizzas and brought them back to nursery. This first-hand experience of how a restaurant worked led to the children organising their own pizza restaurant in a corner of the room, creating pizzas from play dough and using pizza delivery boxes. The whole sequence of their interests – the pretend cooking, the actual visit and the play that followed – was captured in photos and shared with the children's families.

Focus children in Garfield reception class

The reception team have three focus children each week and the detailed planning for those days is led by the interests of those children. Every child has the opportunity to be a focus child each term. The process starts at the end of the previous week when a sheet goes home with next week's focus children about 'Ruby's Special Week'. Parents are invited to complete the sheet with their child and include the current interests of their son or daughter, any recent family events and subjects on which their child has been keen to ask questions.

The week starts with this sheet and from the Monday, each reception teacher, supported by their colleague in that class, plans immediately on the basis of this child's expressed interests. The longest gap in reacting to a child's interests is a day later, for events that need a bit of prior organisation. (Up until 2009 the team made plans for the following week on the basis of this week. However, they found that the gap was enough that individual interests had already moved on.) Each of the focus children is featured on the special board in reception class. Their chosen interests and experiences are documented on the board, building up over the week.

The Garfield children enjoy free flow, with the exception of come-together times for each class at the beginning and end of each morning and the afternoon. The personal projects of the focus children are especially highlighted in these shared group times.

On the morning of my visit I watched as one reception key group enjoyed looking at a sequence of photos projected onto the screen, showing a recent trip out to the park. Jaleel, who was the focus child, had been interested in making a river. Through the photo presentation, Jaleel chose to sit comfortably on the adult's lap, as they talked through the narrative, photo by photo. The practitioner added a few open-ended questions and other children recalled the highlights of this outing for everyone. Then Jaleel outlined his plan for the day: to explore how to make dirty water clean. The practitioner had found a science book with a possible experiment and Jaleel chose his companions for this exploration.

Close adult involvement is focused on the chosen enterprises of the focus children. A narrative observation early in the week and continued close attention guides the adults in their involvement in the play, conversation and chosen special experiences of the focus children. What has been learned from each child's special week forms part of their ongoing personal record, in which the team continue to highlight the developing skills and next steps for this child.

Each child's special week is also written up into two pages (laminated), with selected photos organised into their special learning story. Headed 'Ruby's Week', this account belongs to the child and family and highlights the future, as well as capturing the special experiences of the week. The child's teacher writes brief personal comments led by wording like: 'Ruby, I noticed on Monday that you really enjoyed … (what the adult helped to organise)' and 'You showed me (or other people) that you could...'. The two page record summarises the events with, 'In your special week, you...' as well as the adult's view, 'I was especially impressed with how you…'. In friendly, straightforward language (which can be read out loud to the child and shared with parents) the record suggests next steps, such as, 'Maybe you would like to...' or 'I will help you with…'.

Leading the key person approach

Childminders have to face and resolve many of the issues experienced by early years practitioners who work in group provision. However, additional issues arise in group provision, because the key person approach needs to be established as a consistent pattern of practice – sometimes over a large setting. To assess how the key person approach works in your setting see the questionnaire on page 35.

A system that works for children

The senior team in group provision have to establish an atmosphere that supports the key person approach. Managers have to know the statutory requirements of the EYFS but, of course, the rationale given to staff is not that 'we have to do it'. The explanation, and continued support, for the importance of close relationships with children and families rests on the developmental knowledge described in the first section of this book. Reflection on how best to establish and maintain a key person approach leads a senior team to consider many aspects of how their provision is run. At any point as you read through this section, you might like to look at the questionnaire on page 35 and consider where your setting stands on the system that backs up the key person approach.

Look closer: Kennet Day Nursery
The senior team of Kennet have considered how best to place a key person approach at the centre of their practice. One decision was to make the role of key person central to the job description for all practitioners.

- **From the outset it is clear to applicants for posts at Kennet that in order to be the key person in the nursery for some children you will establish and maintain a high-quality relationship with these children and oversee their development in key areas: emotional, intellectual, social, physical and linguistic. You will establish and maintain good two-way communication with their parents/carers on all aspects of the child's development and care, bridging the gap between nursery and home. You will support other staff with the care and development of their key children and families, acting as a buddy for other staff members and supporting with the planning and communication for the best outcomes for children.**

- **This role is further clarified in the description of the responsibilities of the post: being the key person for**

Links to your practice

The rationale for any particular way of organising the key person approach has to rest on ensuring it works for the children. No early years provision, nor any member of the workforce, should choose their priorities by what seems easier, quicker or more efficient for adults. Practical issues or concerns have to be resolved with the children's best interests at the centre of any decision.

The senior team of Randolph Beresford Early Years Centre support a large staff group in their daily practice and thoughtful review of that practice. They sum up their approach with: "The child first; everyone else afterwards".

Both sole practitioners and teams can benefit from watchwords to guide choices when you have to balance the needs and preferences of adults as well as children's wellbeing. You can still be flexible, but not to the point where young children slip down the list of priorities.

individual children is the first core duty in the list of tasks. The role is briefly outlined, so that it is very clear that practitioners are responsible for the beginning of the relationship with families and that this close contact continues day by day.

- The Kennet senior team also made the decision to place a 'caring attitude' at the top of the list of 'skills and abilities' necessary for the practitioners who wish to join the team. The job description highlights that Kennet does not accept an interpretation of key working that rests on an impersonal approach.

The Kennet senior team, like the other settings I visited for this book, are equally clear that they are responsible for supporting practitioners in the role as a key person: to be ready to listen, continue to explain and explore what key working means in practice and to work together to resolve any dilemmas.

In Kennet, the relationship with families usually stretches over many years, since children tend to start with the nursery as babies and stay until they leave to go to a local reception class. Many day nurseries, although not all, have this kind of sustained relationship with families over much of early childhood.

When do you choose the key person?

The senior team of any group provision needs to decide how a key person is chosen for each family. The most usual approach is for the senior team to identify the practitioner who will be the best key person, as soon as it is clear that a family will join the setting. The key person needs to be in place ready for the home visit or a personalised visit to your setting. The advantage of this system is that the key person becomes familiar to the child and family from the very beginning.

Obviously, potential key persons need to have space in their key group. Also any practitioner needs to have settled into the job. Even experienced, newly arrived practitioners should have time to become familiar with this provision before becoming the key person with their first family.

I have read about a few nurseries who wait until the child is well into the settling-in period. Practitioners observe whether the child gravitates towards a particular practitioner, who then becomes the key person for the child and family. The advantage of this approach is that the child is able to make an active choice, although not all show a clear preference. The disadvantage is that a named individual is not in place to start the personal relationship with a child and parent(s) from the very beginning. There is also the potential problem of an uneven spread of children across available practitioners. The EYFS does not specify the detail of how the key person system works, so managers and their team have to weigh up what

works best for children and families. My preference would be for assigning a key person and then making a discreet change, if a baby or child makes a strong attachment to a different practitioner.

Dealing with flexible attendance

The system backing the key person approach sometimes has to deal with a high level of complexity. I have been very impressed by the organisational juggling act that senior teams attempt for the best interests of young children. You have to do the best possible under your operating circumstances.

- In part-time provision, there are more children on the register than are present each day. However, provision that offers full-time places often has a proportion of children who attend only for some days. Parents have increasingly opted for the chance to work part- rather than full-time, with the consequence of more part-time places.

- Assigning the key person has to avoid the situation in which one practitioner has an unrealistic number of key children, even on only some days of the week. Slight imbalances may be redressed by practitioners who have fewer key children on that day or session, or possibly none at all. These practitioners do not suddenly take on new key children. In good team working, they look out for colleagues who today have a full complement of key babies or children.

■ It is also important to fit the attendance pattern of the child to the working pattern of the practitioner, if she or he does not work full-time. Some elements of this can be eased by having the partner key person on a working pattern that complements that of the main key person.

■ In a partner or buddying system, the second named practitioner becomes familiar with the child and family. She or he is a known face and ready to step in when the main key person is not present. In full daycare the shift system for practitioners, and a long day for some children, means that the partner is involved with the child and family on a fairly regular basis.

■ Partner key working is also one way of addressing the practical problems arising from term-time and full-year members of staff. This longstanding problem of different terms of service for teachers has very occasionally been resolved by setting up a centre with identical terms of service, regardless of the professional route taken by team members.

Flexibility has become something of a buzz word applied to early years provision, especially when politicians want highly flexible registered childcare to support parents with diverse working patterns. This stance has been continued by the current coalition government. The possible advantages of a flexible outlook over the years of early childhood nevertheless bring some complications. Best practice for children is undermined when a high level of flexibility over attendance is driven by an adult agenda. It is noticeable that the statutory school system is not required to offer equivalent flexibility within its normal hours of operation.

Early years provision should not offer a 'one size fits all' pattern in terms of hours or days for every family. However, some official pronouncements about high flexibility disregard the likely consequences for young children, if they attend even a single form of provision in an unpredictable pattern – from their perspective. My professional concerns have been echoed by early years practitioners and managers in conversations over recent years. Young children can be relatively resilient, but they struggle to settle when a variable pattern of attendance means young boys and girls cannot become familiar with the supportive routines and flow of a session or day. This security of emotional wellbeing is necessary to support sustained learning in the broader sense. When many children follow variable patterns in the name of flexibility for the adults, then the children are unlikely to enjoy the sustained companionship of familiar peers, which is the foundation for friendships.

Who do you choose?

Your aim is to find a good fit between the family and key person. Managers and senior teams say that sometimes the earliest contacts with a family give hints for choosing the key person from available team members.

Usually the same practitioner would be the key person for siblings – unless parents explained a preference for a different person. One possible reason might be that they felt that twins, or children very close in age, would benefit from a degree of separation – perhaps because one child tends to speak for the other. In early years provision children will often move between rooms and, under those circumstances, siblings might start with the same key person but have periods of time when they are not in the same key group. Under those circumstances, it is professional to look for ways for the two key persons involved with a family to work well together and ensure that a parent does not end up having to pass on family information twice, but also that nothing falls between the cracks. It makes sense for the two practitioners to talk with the parent(s) at an early stage and together decide what will work best.

The choice of a key person will have to recognise that practitioners sometimes live in the same neighbourhood as they work, and possibly grew up there, too. You want clear boundaries between personal and professional life. So it is inappropriate for a practitioner to be the key person for a parent who is a close friend in non-work life, or who is a relative. Some settings offer places to the children of staff and, it is not feasible for a practitioner to be the key person for their own baby or child.

If possible the senior team will aim to have a key person who speaks the home language of a family. A child, especially a very young one, can then be reassured by a familiar language. However, even diverse teams will have their limits in a linguistically diverse neighbourhood. A bilingual key person should nevertheless support the child in learning English as the main general form of spoken communication.

Otherwise, it is questionable practice to match a key person to a family on ethnic group, culture or faith – whatever the identity of the family or key person – and the same applies for sex or sexual orientation. Best equality practice within early years will not be to try to place 'like with like' as a matter of course. Such a system would give the impression that practitioners are unable to relate to a fellow adult whom they judge to be different from themselves in a key feature of identity.

The senior team needs to provide additional guidance if they judge that some practitioners need that support. Perhaps a key person is uncertain about the practical implications of the family faith and feels uneasy about asking the parent. Maybe several practitioners have a misplaced belief that fathers should be treated very differently from mothers and this outlook is disrupting the relationship. Alternatively, maybe the key person misunderstands and thinks that equality practice means treating everyone exactly the same. (For more about equality see Lindon, 2012b and 2012c.)

A family may ask for a particular key person, on the basis of preferring, or not wanting, a practitioner of a given ethnic group, faith or sex. Partnership with parents would require the senior team to listen and to understand the basis of this request. Each case would be taken on its merits, but it is very unlikely to be appropriate to agree to a preference based on a family's wish to avoid a practitioner of a different ethnic group, or faith, to the family. Similar issues arise if a family very clearly wants to avoid

a male practitioner. If parents feel strongly that they do not want a male to be close to their daughter or son, then they can opt for a female childminder (again see Lindon, 2006b and 2008).

Enabling a positive relationship

The system supporting the key person approach needs to be organised in ways that respect and support the entire life of a positive relationship with families. This relationship starts with first contact and ends when children and the family leave your provision. Sometimes the narrative of this relationship lasts no more than a couple of terms, but sometimes the relationship lasts many years.

Some aspects of first contact are discussed from page 6. This section expands those points from the perspective of a consistent approach, ensured by the senior team. Best practice is to ensure that the first serious conversation between parents and the key person is a personal event, not a case of milling around in a large information event for many parents. Many settings offer a home visit, because this approach is more personal and appropriate for families with young children. The point about arranging a home visit, or if the parent(s) prefer, a first significant meeting at the setting, is to begin the relationship well.

It is important that the senior team guide the expectations of practitioners about the content of the home visit. It is unwise to

Even a successful process, of first contact and settling, benefits from reflection about what is working well and what might benefit from adjustment.

- What do you need to know and understand from the family to start a personalised approach to their child or children?

- What do they need to know and understand about the service that you offer?

- How much needs to be clarified at the very first contact?

- What can be left as part of follow-up conversations and a handover of material?

- What do you write down, so that it can be handed to each family?

- Are you alert to the possibility that some parents are ill-at-ease with reading and writing? There is a hidden problem of adults who are not confident in their literacy skills, but are not necessarily living with dyslexia.

- What about the practical issues when you work in a neighbourhood with a considerable number of different home languages? It may be feasible to get your main written material translated into the main family languages. However, in some areas with high levels of diversity, this can be a daunting task. You also need to ensure that any translation is done alongside someone who understands early years provision. Literal translation can miss the meaning.

Links to your practice

Early years group provision operates in different ways. The senior team of full year settings have most usually established a pattern of steady entry, so that no key person is settling more than one child at a time.

When provision runs only in term time, the senior team sometimes has to resolve historical patterns of entry. Provision that accepts children from three years of age, and increasingly the twos, has to organise a staggered entry, even when there is a significant exit of children at some points of the year. Children are still young, even at the oldest end of the EYFS, and it is not responsible to have large numbers of four- or five-year-olds starting in a batch in reception class.

have unrealistic hopes about how much can be said to fellow adults, and remembered, in one sitting. It is also appropriate that the senior team establish a consistent pattern for home visits. I have talked with many teams where it is usual for two people to go on the home visit, one of whom is definitely the key person. The advantage of having two people is that one practitioner can talk with the parent(s) and the other can focus on the baby or child. I have also known the decision for two practitioners to attend any home visit to be in response to personal safety issues in some neighbourhoods.

Over the course of the home visit and settling-in period for each child, the key person needs to have covered all the main issues concerning the provision on offer. Details will include parents' signatures on the relevant consent forms such as taking children out and about for ordinary trips in the local neighbourhood, or consent for emergency medical treatment. This consent should be fully informed in the sense that parents need to know what is meant by the phrases on a consent form and be given further explanation if the key person realises that any parent seems unclear. If several parents seem puzzled – which you find by bringing together the experiences of several practitioners in their key person role – then maybe the wording is not written in straightforward language. The same awareness applies to any materials you share with parents.

The senior teams of all the settings I visited for this book had thought carefully about first impressions for parents who were considering taking up a place at the nursery, centre or pre-school. Home visits did not happen until the family had accepted a place and prior to that time every effort was made to ensure that parents were clear about the main features of what was on offer. In some settings, the manager or someone else from the senior team does the walk-round tour with any parents who are considering the provision. Later on there is a good chance that parents will realise that their key person is not making a personally directed criticism when talking about the need to arrive on time to pick up a child. Practitioners will be understanding about emergencies but otherwise the times have been agreed. Parents can be courteously reminded that the policy here is that everyone switches off their mobile before they enter the building. This key person is not expressing a one-off objection to this parent's use of the mobile phone.

Look closer: Randolph Beresford Early Years Centre

The head has a meeting with each family before parents make the final decision to ask for a place, and before the home visit by the key person. The aim of this conversation is that parents have accurate expectations about the centre.

- **The head covers the settling-in process and outlines that every parent is expected to clear a period of two weeks to enable them steadily to ease their child into the unfamiliar situation.**

It is also made clear, in a friendly way, that children play in this centre, which means they go outside a very great deal. Children will get messy from enjoyable indoor as well as outdoor activities. They will have the occasional play-related accident – as attentive as the staff are in taking good care of all children.

■ The centre has many well-illustrated wall displays, with straightforward written explanation. So it is easy for parents new to the centre, or to early years provision in general, to grasp what a normal day looks like here.

■ Parents are also told about the centre policy and practice on behaviour and the basic ground rules that apply to everyone – adults as well as children – once they are within the centre.

. . . .

Look closer: Kennet Day Nursery

The senior team reflected on how the important relationship with a family begins. At the time of my visit, they had not long reviewed their induction materials. They considered that the pattern of the home visit was perhaps over-weighted towards what the key person needed to tell parents – rather than relaxed time to start the process of getting to know the parent(s) and baby or child. Consequently they decided to send the information pack to a family in good time before the home visit. At that time, the family is also sent descriptive information about the nursery in the handbook.

■ A 'welcome' letter is sent when a family has a confirmed place in the nursery. This one page sheet offers a home visit and explains briefly that parents will settle their baby or child into nursery, with the support of their key person. The letter also explains a few practical details, such as choosing a family photo for the nursery and what parents need to provide for their baby or child.

■ The key person assigned to the family then makes the telephone call to introduce her/himself and arrange a day and time. Kennet has found, like many settings, that most parents appreciate the option of a home visit. But, should they prefer, this first meeting can happen in the nursery.

■ Ideally parents complete the information pack before the home visit. This request is grounded in the clear wish to understand 'your' baby or child and their family life.

Like many settings, in Kennet the key person makes the home visit with a colleague. The focus is on a conversational approach with opportunities for parents to ask or answer questions about the information they have completed about their baby or child and any queries about the handbook and contract for the nursery place. The aim of the home visit is to build a detailed picture of the child and family, to sense how this parent feels about leaving their baby or child. The key person takes the opportunity to show that the nursery, led by her or him, really wants to know how best to reassure this family that Kennet will take good individual care of their son or daughter.

The key person has two reminder sheets to ensure that they have covered significant issues during the home visit. So for example, if it has not arisen, the key person will describe how the Day Book works. This documents patterns of sleep, feeding, nappy changes or toilet training and a personal highlight of the child's day. The Day Book ensures communication between the key person and home. This daily summary report travels to and fro until a baby is a year old or for a period of three to four months when young children start as toddlers. Other practical issues about the place, such as consent forms, are covered within the first visit to the nursery in the process of settling in.

Food for thought

Parents, or other family carers, who have recently experienced your induction and settling-in process are uniquely qualified to give you constructive feedback on how it went for them. This valuable source of information is often overlooked.

Within the friendly working relationship which you should have established, most of those fellow-adults will feel comfortable that you would really like to hear their informed views, rather than a bland "it was all fine".

Depending on the families with whom you work, you could have a focused conversation or a simple questionnaire. You do not want lots of questions. An example is below. (If you work as a childminder, just reword it by substituting 'me' and 'I' for 'us' and 'we'.)

> Now that you and your child are settled with us, we would welcome hearing about the early days and weeks from your point of view. Looking back now:
>
> ■ What worked well for you and your baby or child?
>
> ■ Is there anything that you would have liked to have known at an earlier stage? Or have explained in a different way?
>
> ■ Is there anything that was clear for you, but you think might puzzle some other parents?
>
> ■ Is there anything that would have made those early days easier for you and your baby or child?

It is unrealistic to expect that parents will take on board every detail about your unfamiliar service, how it works and any boundaries to what you offer. If you start the relationship well, parents feel comfortable to ask further questions and the key person feels at ease to address any misunderstanding which arises.

■ Even provision that sounds much the same will have different patterns of working. If parents are new to early years provision in general, they may be unsure about what is usual.

■ However, parents whose child has already attended some kind of early years provision may reasonably work on the assumption that what they experienced in the previous nursery or playgroup is what happens here.

■ Maybe a parent is sure someone said the nursery would provide nappies, when families are expected to bring their own.

■ Perhaps an overall message of wanting to be flexible with family preferences has been interpreted by this parent that the nursery has committed to agreeing to every request.

■ The key person may need to deal with requests that, if followed, would mean serious disruption, such as a very rigid schedule for the baby or a parent who wishes to determine whether a child goes outdoors each day.

The continuity of the key person approach is interrupted if a practitioner leaves the setting. So long as the staff group is relatively stable, then this change has to be approached as a transition for adults and children alike. The relationship with the new key person needs to be introduced in the same way careful way as the first entry of the family to the setting. If a senior team has to deal with a high turnover of staff, the problems arising from regular change, and an attempt to understand the reasons, has to be tackled to protect good early years practice, whatever the system organised for the key person approach.

Some settings cater for the full early childhood age range and decisions about organisation can mean that the key person will change over the years that a family attends this provision – but not necessarily. Very small nurseries may work with the full age range within one key group, so practitioners could form close relationships with key children ranging from babies up to young fives. Some larger, full age range nurseries have established mixed-age family grouping. The senior team ensures that the system meets, or exceeds, the correct number of practitioners given the ages of the children. So, for some group provision the key person relationship lasts until the child and family move on to another setting.

The advantage of mixed-age grouping is that children benefit from contact with younger and older girls and boys. This approach also eases contact between siblings. It is always tricky to talk about what is natural for childhood. But in general family and extended family life does not limit young children to interaction with a narrow band of age peers. However, many settings with children in age-related rooms as their home base organise a flow to the day in which the ages are able to go visiting or mix regularly in the garden.

Much as in a family, the different ages within a full span key group often appreciate time with their age peers. Best early years practice – for the EYFS and other frameworks within the UK – is to create child-friendly routines around generous time for child-initiated experiences, accessing a well-resourced learning environment. Under these circumstances mobile over twos will head off to play with their chosen companions – see the example below.

Look closer: Start Point Sholing Early Years Centre

This early years centre offers full daycare (from babies) and a sessional nursery class for three-to-fives within the same centre. The key person approach in the daycare facility is based on each practitioner having key children across the full age range from babyhood. The large space is divided into areas, but not into separate age based rooms. Individual children experience continuity with their key person across their whole stay with Start Point Sholing.

The senior team within Start Point Sholing is very aware that best practice within the day nursery depends on a secure knowledge of child development across the full age range of early childhood. The team has a nought to two lead practitioner who is able to offer additional professional support for key persons who would welcome further guidance with the very youngest age group.

The key person approach has been developed alongside a full team awareness of the environment created for the children. The leaders of each team were keen to create a shared learning environment. In the autumn before my visit, a section of internal wall was replaced with a concertina screen door, which remains open for most of the day. Young children from the day nursery area move freely into the nursery class area and into the indoor-outdoor free-flow that operates there. The day nursery has its own door to the garden and mobile toddlers and children also use that way to access the garden. The team has put effort into making this system

work. All practitioners remain alert, and communicate with each other, to ensure that younger children have an adult close by.

The over-threes from the day nursery spend much of their day, out of choice, with their age peers in the nursery class. The positive consequence has been that resources suitable to this age group are not duplicated between the day nursery and nursery class. The day nursery resources can be weighted rather more towards the younger children, although much of the equipment is common across the age range; children use similar resources in a different way.

In both areas the space is divided into smaller areas, some of which have a particular focus in terms of resources. The smaller spaces also allow small groups of children, who choose to play together, to have relatively protected space in which they can spread out with their chosen focus. Both indoor areas use furniture, larger play equipment, the storage systems, drapery and floor covering to create distinct areas. The day nursery has created a special area for babies, known as the Safe Haven, located at the top end of the space and surrounded by low, see-through room dividers. Entry and exit is by a wooden a gate which mobile toddlers and children are able to open and shut. The aim is to have a protected space in which young babies can be on the floor and an adult is with them. Older children are welcome to come into the Safe Haven and they understand that here is not the place for speedy or vigorous play.

Supporting transitions

In the many group settings who organise groups/rooms by age the senior team has to manage the internal transitions. Even if the age bands, and home based rooms, are kept fairly broad, a child who starts as a baby will have more than one move between base rooms. Best practice is that these moves are treated with care as internal transitions for the baby or child and family. Some settings offer another home visit at this time of change for a young child and parent(s) and the family has chance to talk with the existing and next key person. Relaxed visits are also organised for children to meet their new key person and become familiar, over a period of time, with their new room and some new faces of other children.

Look closer: Randolph Beresford Early Years Centre (RBEYC)

For some years, the key person approach within the RBEYC was that young children moved from the under threes unit as a group with their key person. The rationale was that children had a sustained relationship throughout their time at the centre. In a full review of practice it was decided that, on balance, the system was not working as well as possible for children.

One issue was that only a relatively small proportion of children in this large centre start as toddlers (the youngest are about 18 months) and continue until they leave for reception class. If the children moved as a whole key group, there was a possibility that they would not make friends from the much large number of children who join the centre at three-years-old.

The move is now treated carefully as an internal transition.

- At least a term before the older twos will move into the three-to-fives part of the centre, they and their parent(s) know which practitioner will become their key person.

- These young children finally move when it makes sense for them and do not have to fit the usual entry times for three-year-olds who first join RBEYC for the nursery class. Close attention is paid to current key groups in the relevant three-to-fives room, so that no group has to welcome a lot of new faces at a time.

- The key person in the under-threes room considers the friendship groups that children have developed in that part of the centre. Young children are never moved as single individuals; they always make the move with a few friends – familiar faces in the new room.

- However, the children also enjoy a lot of visiting in the slow run-up to the final move. The under-threes in the centre have their own outdoor space but are able to see the garden area of the over-threes. It is not unusual for practitioners to take the younger ones out into the larger garden, so this outdoor space becomes familiar.

- Children make a series of regular visits to the three-to-fives room which they will eventually join and become familiar with their next key person, the layout of the new room and the routines.

- The current and next key person keep in close communication and discuss what is working best for individual children. They decide together when the current key person will take children to the three-to-fives room and also when the new key person will visit children in their current under threes room.

- The next key person is busy learning about the personal preferences and current development of the children, aiming to provide continuity, as well as the positive anticipation for these very young children of joining the 'big children'. The two practitioners also discuss whether children will want and benefit from visits 'back' to the under-threes room.

A few nurseries choose, and manage successfully, to have each key person 'travel' through the age rooms of a nursery with their key children. I have learned a great deal from senior teams who support travelling key groups. The advantage of having key groups travel is that it offers continuity to children and families. Neither the child nor the parent(s) have to develop a relationship with the new key person, probably at least twice in a birth-to-five years range nursery or centre.

For this pattern of organisation to work the rationale must continue to be clear to all team members. Even in stable staff groups there will be some changes and any practitioners new to this setting need to be aware of and fully understand the reasons why they travel with their children. Of course, any senior team needs to address that all practitioners commit to the key person approach and the role, whatever the system that is organised for this setting.

· ·

Look closer: Kennet Day Nursery

In Kennet the under-threes are in two groups: Minnows (babies and young toddlers up to about 20 months) and Dragonflies (from about 20 months to three years of age). The nursery team developed an under-threes unit approach when they had an internal wall removed and replaced with a low-level wooden screen and gate. The mobile toddlers and twos are able to move between the two spaces as a coherent learning environment and the very youngest are safe in the Minnows space.

This reorganisation of the physical environment enabled a change in how the key person approach worked. The most likely event now is that toddlers move from Minnows with their key person. After this change it was noticed that the children who had moved into the Dragonflies base area did not want to return to the Minnows space for personal attention, because their key person had moved with them. During my visit, I noticed how young children opened the wooden gate and went into Minnows in a purposeful way. Very young boys and girls set off to have a chat with someone in that space, to settle down with interesting materials on the floor or to ask for a particular play resource that they knew, from experience, was stored in a given cupboard.

The Kennet senior team consider carefully how to assign a key person to a family about to join the setting and part of that decision is to maintain key groups that do not have too wide an age range. Transitions between rooms are still taken on an individual basis and a decision reached on the details of each case. Kingfishers (3-5s) are on the same site just across the garden, but not in the same main building. Occasionally a key person and children have moved across to Kingfishers together. One practitioner was in this position with his key group during the time that I visited. In this case, the practitioner will stay with the Kingfishers team until all his key children have left and then he will return to the under threes team. However, it is more usual that the key person from Dragonflies will support children and families to make the transition to a new key person in Kingfishers.

This move is treated as an important step and the existing key person organises several visits to the Kingfishers' base area and helps the child to become familiar with their key person. I could see on my visits, that the older twos are already familiar with the staff of the Kingfishers team, because the children sometimes spend time in the garden space especially set up for the over-threes. The nearly-threes look very confident in this outdoor environment and have already headed round the garden corner to check out the Kingfishers space – and sometimes to help themselves to resources that they need in the outdoor space.

Nevertheless, the children's move between the under-threes group and the three-to-fives group is approached as a step-by-step process and parents are kept informed. A letter to the family lets them know that the move will be soon and gives the name of the new key person. Parents are invited to visit Kingfishers and meet the key person. The invitation to visit is still made if the same key person is transferring with the key group. The aim is to start the relationship in the over threes room and to deal afresh with any expectations. Not unusually for nurseries, some parents in Kennet – not all – expect that the move to Kingfishers will bring a more formal, school-type approach. Since Kennet follows best EYFS practice, the approach remains a consistent focus on play, conversation and generous scope for children's child-initiated play (see Lindon, 2010a).

A Transition Record is completed, which supplements conversations between practitioners. This record means that the new key person has an up-to-date written record of the family information, child's health, personal care needs including issues like how they manage in the toilet and food or other preferences. The record also covers their current interests and play preferences and close relationships with adults or children.

The new key person is poised to build a close relationship and parents are offered a home visit if they would like this opportunity, as well as visits to Kingfishers to become familiar with this area and other

members of the team besides their new key person. The Transition Record is still completed, if the key person moves with their key group of children from Dragonflies into Kingfishers. An existing key person still needs to share that personal knowledge with his/her new colleagues in the room.

My understanding has also grown from conversation with senior teams who have, on reflection, returned to age-based groups and a focus on supporting the consequent internal transition.

- The disadvantage, from the organisational perspective, is that travelling key groups across the full age range can raise difficulties for balancing the staff team and the point at which a practitioner returns to the beginning of the age range. It also creates a situation in which the room team for any part of the setting continues to change.

- In some cases, this pattern is not experienced as a major issue, but sometimes the continued readjustment to adult working partners can be problematic. If the adult room teams do not gel, then the overall experience may be less positive for the children.

- Some early years practitioners are genuinely more comfortable and professionally skilled with one age group than another. Some experienced practitioners have a real flair for being with babies and young toddlers. Some equally committed practitioners feel better attuned to the over-threes.

- Within a team covering the full age range, everyone needs to respect the ages, which they do not personally cover. With respect for the children must also come respect for colleagues who spend time with those babies or children.

The key issue is, of course, whether any form of organisation operates in the interests of the children. In some group settings, the balanced decision is that travelling groups, or a full age range key group in a single birth-to-five space, work to the benefit of children. Any remaining issues or uncertainties are covered through internal support for the team and continued professional development. However, sometimes the travelling key groups are judged not to work well enough for the children.

The key person role is a close personal relationship: an emotional bond between the key person, the child and the parent(s) or other family member who is a primary carer. Unjustified dismissal of a proper key person is sometimes underpinned with a general comment that 'staff get too attached to the children'. Usually when I hear this phrase, it is a warning that the senior team is unwilling to address the sensitive issues that underpin a proper

key person approach (see more about adopting a personal approach on page 14). However, within my visits related to this book I heard some carefully expressed concerns about the possibility of over-attachment. I describe these important practice issues in the next two paragraphs.

It is especially challenging for a key person working with vulnerable and chaotic families to maintain the balance needed in the key person role. Genuine emotional commitment to the child and family has to coexist with a professional detachment that enables difficult conversation and tough decisions, especially if safeguarding is an issue. Undoubtedly, other professions like social workers and family support workers have to achieve this balance. However, those other professionals do not see the family as often, or necessarily over such a long period of time, as early years practitioners. Nor are they so closely involved with the children. It is also true that members of those professions are more likely to have been specifically trained for this role than many early years practitioners, even the more experienced members of the workforce.

Sometimes the senior team in a setting catering for vulnerable families judges that having the same key person with a family, over what could be as long as five years, is asking too much of individual staff – even with full back-up and continued professional development. Some managers decide, on balance, that children are better supported when they are able to form a close relationship with more than one key person over the span of their time with the setting.

Attachment within the family

Whatever the organisational system, practitioners in the key person role should always bear in mind that children need to form and maintain a strong emotional bond within their own family. Young children sometimes spend their early childhood happily attending the same nursery, and sometimes their entire childhood with the same childminder. However, when they leave, their own family needs to be the continuity in the child's life.

- In some families, a variety of pressures and adult problems mean that very young children have not formed a strong attachment to their parent(s). Under those circumstances, it may not help the child in the end if they form a very strong bond with a single key person, because they travel together through the setting. The child may then experience serious loss when they leave for reception class, because they have not experienced that it is possible to become close to a small number of trustworthy and caring adults.

- Again, under these circumstances the senior team will be focused on ways to support the parents to focus on their children, with such help as is possible for resolving those social or personal problems that are getting in the way.

A related issue has to be considered when the youngest group in a setting, or a specialist support group, has a high proportion of children from vulnerable families. If these key groups then travel together into the three-to-fives section or the main group, then the children lose the benefits of close contact with peers from less vulnerable families.

Family stress will frequently have an impact on the development of young children, perhaps in their level of communication skills or their ability to guide their own behaviour in ways that their age peers can usually manage. Part of the advantage of early years provision can be that children, whose family experiences have been unfavourable, can mix with young girls and boys whose lives are far less chaotic.

The key person approach means that a close relationship should have developed with the child and the family. It is appropriate to recognise the ending of this closeness in a way that looks back with pleasure at joint times and shows confidence that all will be well in the next stage. The senior team sets the emotional tone that, of course, the event is marked, people do not just say goodbye and that is that.

The key person will ensure that a child's individual learning journey is fully up-to-date. The usual pattern would be that this personal document would be given to the child and family, along with any remaining personal artwork or models. In consultation with parents, the key person would organise any kind of summary record that goes to the next setting and key person, if the child will still be within the EYFS early childhood span.

The key person needs to lead on the gradual and friendly transition for this child and family to somewhere and someone else. I have encountered very thoughtful transition arrangements between nursery and into reception which have been supported by the efforts of the key person and the senior team in making contact with other settings, some of whom are more welcoming than others.

Many settings have a party or other social event. If children leave you in groups, perhaps to go to reception class, you may have joint parties. However, sometimes children will leave as individuals, perhaps because the family is moving home. Photos of this event will be provided for the family and children given the opportunity to take photos of anything in the setting that is important to them, so they could keep a permanent record.

Look closer: Start Point Sholing Early Years Centre

The places that I visited while writing this book included both smaller and large group provision. The settings shared many features in how the senior team organised and supported a key person approach. Large children's centres like Start Point Sholing tend to experience other practical aspects as a result of the range of services that are delivered within the building.

Families have sometimes become familiar with the centre before their child joins the day nursery or nursery class provision. They and their child may have enjoyed facilities like stay and play sessions or made regular visits to other parts of the centre for specialist or community services. A level of familiarity is useful so that families do not find a large centre confusing. However, families who have attended other facilities still receive a full introduction to what is a new service – day nursery or nursery class – at Start Point Sholing.

By the time a child leaves to go to reception class some parents have had a long relationship stretching over several years, especially if several siblings have attended the centre. Some parents have been able to access the broad range of support services that are delivered within a large centre. The Start Point team are aware that they can have become what they view as a professional member of the extended family. The transition of children and parents to another setting, most likely reception class, can feel like the end of an important era. Each child and family deserves and benefits from careful attention to this time of transition. However, some parents may feel that they are leaving a very supportive group of people and transition is an emotional wrench for the adult. Under these circumstances, the centre team and the key persons are particularly attentive to the experience of parents as well as of their children.

Dealing with practice issues

Best practice for professionalism in early years is that practitioners become close to their key children and that the children view their key person as their special adult and safe place. The senior team is responsible for creating and maintaining an organisational system that supports the key person approach. But the manager and the senior team are also responsible for dealing with issues about practice.

Uncertainties that affect the whole setting need to be raised in team meetings, if necessary more than once. Some issues may be particular to a room team and are then best discussed with these practitioners.

Individual, regular supervision sessions with practitioners can be the time to raise key person practice, as well as any other issues.

It is equally important that the senior team is easily available for individual practitioners to start a conversation, even informally or for a senior practitioner to raise points about the relationship with a child, parent or both.

The different types of early years provision are busy places and the senior team has a wide range of obligations. The teams in all the settings I visited for this book made serious efforts to review and refresh how the key person approach worked in the setting as a whole. But they were also available to talk with individual practitioners about their role as a key person and to listen to practical concerns.

In recent studies (Elfer et al., 2003) and less contemporary reports (Bain and Barnett, 1986), researchers describe how practitioners too often have very limited opportunity to talk about their experiences of being a key person to young children and their family. Sometimes the research context appears to be the first chance for practitioners to talk in any detail about what they do in the key person role and what they believe to be the priorities. Juliet Hopkins (1988) explored the worries underlying practitioners' feeling that they should not get too close to the children for whom they were responsible in a day nursery. Staff were concerned there might be an inequality between how children were treated and that young children could become possessive of an adult. These are issues that still concern practitioners, because they go to the heart of a close relationship with young children.

Two decades later Catherine Croft (2009) discussed very similar issues that arose for practitioners in a centre where the key person approach was fully accepted. Her action research project started at a team's professional development day in which practitioners were encouraged to consider personal experiences: their own emotional journey. They then explored their feelings about being a key person, using visual methods like small world play to express issues arising for them from young children's emotional needs and behaviour. Catherine Croft offered support to four practitioners through sessions for reflection in which she contributed her own observations of the key children. Her comments about individual children, and what they might be feeling, helped practitioners to feel that they too could talk about children's emotional life and their own adult reactions. (See Lindon 2012e for more about supervision and reflective practice.)

A central idea in Catherine Croft's action research was the concept of emotional containment, described by Peter Elfer (2006) and Julia Manning-Morton (2006). Young children need to feel confident that they are emotionally and physically safe with their familiar adult – a parent at home and their key person in non-family provision. Children need to be sure that, even if they are expressing strong feelings, such as distress, frustration or anger, this trusted familiar person will not reject them for what they express. On the contrary, that person will show that they recognise the feelings and will help the child to deal with the current emotional collapse. This trusted adult will support – not try to suppress the emotions – and will if necessary contain the child in the safety of their adult arms.

Supporting the practitioners in their role as a key person

These very practical researchers make similar points about how the senior team needs to support children through encouraging

practitioners in the key person role. The senior team are responsible to make the time and to reflect on their own doubts – if they have them – which risk undermining the key person approach. Please think about these issues, which I have now expressed in my own words.

It is professional to care about babies and young children, to be personal and warm with them. Best professional practice with children cannot be emotionally detached.

- A key person should be emotionally committed to their key children, although they will not be as deeply involved as a parent. Their key children are a significant, sustained responsibility – but not 24/7 and not forever.

- Experienced and supported early years practitioners bring the professionalism of sound child development knowledge. They need realistic expectations for the ways in which babies and young children are likely to experience separation and to express their feelings before they have the words.

- Members of the senior team need to be comfortable to talk with practitioners about their key person relationships. The senior team should demonstrate that here it is regarded as professional to express the emotional content of that relationship.

Early years practitioners need a chance for regular confidential discussion – not necessarily very long and with a practical focus. The studies which gave practitioners an opportunity to air their feelings in a safe environment found that this professional discussion helped the move towards greater intimacy for key persons with the children. Practitioners were also very relieved to realise that the concerns they wanted to raise about the key person role were viewed as problems to be understood and resolved, not as professional failures to criticise.

Opportunities for talk and support

Once a practitioner feels able to say in confidence: "I feel so hopeless. Liam sobs whatever I do", then it is more possible for a senior team member to offer support. In an open and supportive conversation, these kinds of issues might arise.

- You explore what is happening, how this key person responds to the distress. Is she or he expecting Liam to cheer up quickly? Are room colleagues supportive, or adding to the problem with comments such as "can't you stop him crying?".

- Professionalism in working with young children means the ability to notice what is happening and avoid jumping to conclusions about children or their parents. Even experienced practitioners sometimes need the support of colleagues to disentangle their own feelings about a child from what that child probably feels in the same situation.

It is possible to feel uneasy, or even that your skills are being challenged, when a baby or child clings tightly. Yet, it is a positive sign that you are the safe base: that a child is confident to turn to you. This normal situation for early childhood is distorted in a mean-spirited atmosphere, where fellow-practitioners criticise with comments such as "you're spoiling her!".

Key persons will not warm to all the children with equal ease. Some young boys or girls, at some time, will irritate a practitioner more easily. The senior team needs to show that it is professional for key persons to realise what they are feeling and to talk it over in confidence. The aim is that the emotion does not get in the way of dealing fairly and warmly with this child.

The emotional atmosphere exerts an influence on observable events. Key persons cannot enable very young children to feel emotionally safe, if those practitioners are uncertain about, or resentful of, normal emotional demands. Very young children cannot regulate their own emotions; they need the support of a familiar adult. Also, emotions are contagious: babies and very young children feel uneasy when they sense a familiar adult feels overwhelmed by events. They feel emotionally rejected if their normal desire for personal attention is reworked in the adult mind as attention-seeking, or a wish for cuddles is dismissed as 'being clingy'.

Key persons are in an intimate relationship with children; professionalism is compatible with affection and physical closeness. Babies and toddlers need to form close attachments. It is irresponsible practice – bordering on a form of emotional abuse – to prevent young children forming a close attachment to a familiar adult, especially when children spend many hours in non-family provision.

Sometimes an emotional distance between adult and child appears to be a way to protect the adults. Young children, even when happy and settled, are emotionally needy; it is a normal state. Some practitioners lack confidence to meet those needs, or their own personal experience leaves them at a loss over how to behave. Then the situation is resolved by pushing emotions to one side and focusing on efficient procedures, inflexible plans and comments such as "we're not supposed to get close; they're not our children".

One objection to a key person approach has been that young children will become 'too attached' to their key person. In group provision this concern has sometimes been the justification for a more administrative view of the key person system or even organising to move practitioners on a regular basis to prevent the development of affectionate relationships.

This area definitely has to be faced and resolved by placing children's needs at the centre of the discussion. In a group setting, key persons should be able to talk with colleagues or the senior team. Nobody must solve the problem by making it hard for young children to form an attachment to their childminder or key person.

Adults – both practitioners and parents – need to resolve the mixed feelings that undoubtedly exist about the key person system. Parents who work long hours may well express concern that their young child is very fond of someone outside the family. However, a similar sensitive issue can be raised in sessional provision when a parent seems less than happy that "he talked about playgroup all weekend."

It is a tough reality to accept as a parent that shared care over early childhood means sharing the affection of your baby or child. Yet children have plenty of affection to go around and parents are helped by a key person who is sensitive to their dilemma. These understandable feelings need to be discussed as fellow adults, with the key person leading on every opportunity to reassure parents.

Young children who spend time away from their family will have some memorable experiences with other people. It is appropriate that key persons are excited with parents about children's interests and achievements. It is also sensitive for key persons to consider whether there are significant developmental milestones that parents may really want to experience themselves. These issues benefit from thought and discussion, if you are part of a team. But I have talked with caring childminders and room teams who are ready to say to a parent: "Heena is so close to walking" or "I'm not sure, do you think Stevie is saying real words?". Such a situation is sensitive and a key person should not be dishonest with parents. However, sometimes it is more considerate to avoid telling a parent immediately that "Heena took her first steps today". It is very possible that Heena will try another mini-stagger when she gets home. There is no easy answer to this dilemma; think about it in your own practice.

The senior team needs to support practitioners to be realistic and establish boundaries when appropriate. Key persons will need to be guided if they set impossibly high standards for themselves and their work.

Early years practitioners need to focus on what is within their responsibility and control. They may be able to offer a friendly adult ear for parents whose life is complicated at the moment. But childminders, or the key person in a group setting, will feel weighed down if they feel responsible for helping in ways that are well outside their remit. Many early years practitioners have neither the time nor the training to offer a counselling role with parents. However, it is important to note that part of the counselling role, in those centres with family support services, is to enable clients to act on their own behalf and not to become dependent on the helper (see Lindon and Lindon, 2008).

The key person approach has non-negotiable features that should be integral to the organisation in any group provision. However, the EYFS does not require an inflexible template for key person practice. This section has covered possible choices over organisation and how the senior team might reach decisions, with the best interests of children at the heart of any choices.

Individual practitioners need to understand the nature of the key person role. But even the most experienced of them have a right to expect support from their senior team and an emotionally warm atmosphere between adults, just as much as for children, in this small community.

Childminders can be isolated because so many work alone. Again it is a professional stance to realise that, however experienced you are, it is wise to have opportunities to talk, in professional confidence, with other people in the early years sector. In some cases the childminding networks and meetings offer this possibility.

Reflecting on the key person approach in your setting

1. The EYFS requires that every setting has a key person approach. Do you?

   ☐ Yes

   ☐ No

   ☐ I don't know

2. Do you have a back-up key person: a named practitioner who is available if the key person is not here that day or to cover a shift system?

   ☐ Yes

   ☐ No

   ☐ I don't know

3. Is it the key person who settles their key baby or child into your setting?

   ☐ Always

   ☐ Most of the time

   ☐ Sometimes

   ☐ After a child is settled

4. After a child is settled, is it still the key person who talks with the child's parent(s)?

   ☐ Usually

   ☐ Sometimes

   ☐ It can be anyone

5. Does a child's key person organise his or her personal records?

   ☐ Usually

   ☐ Sometimes

   ☐ It can be anyone

6. Does the key person attend to the personal care needs of their key babies or children (nappy changing, bottle feeding, toilet training etc.)?

   ☐ Usually

   ☐ Sometimes

   ☐ It can be anyone

7. Does the key person comfort their key children if they are unhappy, ill or otherwise out of sorts?

   ☐ Usually

   ☐ Sometimes

   ☐ It can be anyone

8. How often does each key person have special time with their key children?

   ☐ Once a day

   ☐ Once a week

   ☐ Never

9. Is it the key person who supports key child and family with transitions – to another group or room, or leaving for different provision?

   ☐ Usually

   ☐ Sometimes

   ☐ It can be anyone

Books and websites

Bain, A., Barnett, L. (1986) *The design of a daycare system in a nursery setting for children under five*, The Tavistock Institute of Human Relations, Occasional Paper No. 8.

Croft, C. (2009) *How can a reflective model of support enhance relationships between babies, young children and practitioners*, MA dissertation in Education in Early Childhood: London Metropolitan University.

Department for Education (2012) *Statutory Framework for the Early Years Foundation Stage: Setting the Standards for Learning, Development and Care for Children from Birth to Five* (www.education.gov.uk/schools/teachingandlearning/curriculum/a0068102/early-years-foundation-stage-eyfs).

Early Education (2012) *Development Matters in the Early Years Foundation Stage* (www.education.gov.uk/schools/teachingandlearning/curriculum/a0068102/early-years-foundation-stage-eyfs).

Elfer, P. (2006) 'Exploring children's expressions of attachment in nursery', *European Early Childhood Education Journal* Vol 14, no 2 pages 81-95.

Elfer, P., Goldschmied, E., Selleck, D. (2003) *Key persons in the nursery: building relationships for quality provision*, David Fulton.

Gerhardt, S. (2004) *Why love matters: how affection shapes a baby's brain*, Routledge.

Goldschmied, E., Jackson, S. (2004) *People under three: young children in daycare*. Routledge.

Healy, J. (2004) *Your Child's Growing Mind: Brain Development and Learning from Birth to Adolescence*, Broadway.

Hope, S. (2007) *A nurturing environment for children up to three*, Islington.

Hopkins, J. (1988) 'Facilitating the development of intimacy between nurses and infants in day nurseries', *Early Childhood Development and Care* Vol 33 pages 99-111.

Learning and Teaching Scotland (2010) *Pre-birth to three: positive outcomes for Scotland's children and families* (www.ltscotland.org.uk/earlyyears/prebirthtothree/nationalguidance/index.asp).

Lindon, J. (2006) *Care and caring matter: young children learning through care*, Early Education.

Lindon, J. (2012) *Parents as partners: Positive Relationships in the Early Years*, Practical Pre-School Books.

Lindon, J. (2013) *Child-initiated learning: Positive Relationships in the Early Years*, Practical Pre-School Books.

Lindon, J. (2012a) *Understanding Child Development 0-8 years*, Hodder Education.

Lindon, J. (2012b) *Understanding Children's Behaviour 0-11 years*, Hodder Education.

Lindon, J. (2012c) *Equality and Inclusion in Early Childhood*, Hodder Education.

Lindon, J. (2012d) *Safeguarding and Child Protection 0-8 years*. Hodder Education.

Lindon, J. (2012e) *Reflective Practice and Early Years Professionalism*, Hodder Education.

Lindon, J., Lindon, L. (2008) *Mastering counselling skills*, Palgrave Macmillan.

Manning-Morton, J. (2006a) 'The personal is professional: professionalism and the birth to three practitioner', *Contemporary issues in early childhood*, Volume 7, no 1.

Manning-Morton, J., Thorp, M. (2006b) *Key times: a framework for developing high quality provision for children under three years old*, Open University Press.

National Children's Bureau Everyday Stories (www.everydaystories.org.uk).

Oates, J. (Ed.) (2007) *Attachment Relationships – Quality of Care for Young Children*, London: Bernard Van Leer Foundation (www.bernardvanleer.org).

Tayler, C. (2007) 'The brain, development and learning in early childhood' in Centre for Educational Research and Innovation. *Understanding the Brain: the Birth of a Learning Science Part II* pages 161-183 (www.education.gov.uk/research/data/uploadfiles/DCSF-RW030.pdf).

Tassoni, P. (2008) *The Practical EYFS Handbook*, Heinemann.

Tizard, B. (2009) 'The making and breaking of attachment theory', *The Psychologist October*, Vol 22 no 10 (www.bps.org.uk/thepsychologist).

Weigand, R. (2007) 'Reflective supervision in child care: the discoveries of an accidental tourist', *Zero to Three*, November, Volume 28, no 2, pages 17-22.

Acknowledgements

My thanks to the managers and teams who made me so welcome and agreed to my using examples from my visits: Garfield Children's Centre which includes the reception class of Garfield Primary School (North London), Kennet Day Nursery (Reading), Ladybirds Pre-School (Southampton), Randolph Beresford Early Years Centre (West London), and Start Point Sholing Early Years Centre (Southampton).

A huge thank you to the children in these settings, who were equally welcoming of a visitor in their territory. Any children mentioned in examples have been given fictional names.

I have also benefited from what I learned in recent years from working as a consultant with several nurseries. My continued thanks to Grove House Children's Centre and to Southlands Kindergarten and Crèche whose thoughtfulness about best practice continues to inform my ideas.

Thank you also to Catherine Croft (early years consultant, Thurrock), Peter Elfer (University of Surrey at Roehampton) and Penny Tassoni (early years consultant).

Notes

Notes

Notes